# CARVING TRADITIONAL FISH DECOYS

## With Patterns and Instructions for 17 Projects

### ANTHONY HILLMAN

Dover Publications, Inc.
New York

The author wishes to thank the following for encouragement, advice and some good stories: Reed Tackle, Marshalls Creek, Pa.; Len Guthrie of Cape Taxidermy, Burleigh, N.J.; John Crossley of Tohickon Glass Eye Co., Erwinna, Pa.; The Great Lakes Fish Decoy Collectors and Carvers Association; Ed Clark; and Robert L. Hayden.

Published in Canada by General Publishing Company, Ltd., 30 Lesmill Road, Don Mills, Toronto, Ontario.

*Carving Traditional Fish Decoys: With Patterns and Instructions for 17 Projects* is a new work, first published by Dover Publications, Inc., in 1993.
These patterns and drawings are not to be used for printed reproduction without permission.

Manufactured in the United States of America
Dover Publications, Inc., 31 East 2nd Street, Mineola, N.Y. 11501

**Library of Congress Cataloging-in-Publication Data**

Hillman, Anthony.
    Carving traditional fish decoys : with patterns and instructions for 16 projects / Anthony Hillman.
        p.    cm.
    ISBN 0-486-27500-0 (pbk.)
    1. Fish decoys.   2. Wood-carving—Patterns.   I. Title.
TT199.75.H542   1993
745.593'6—dc20                                                              92-41807
                                                                              CIP

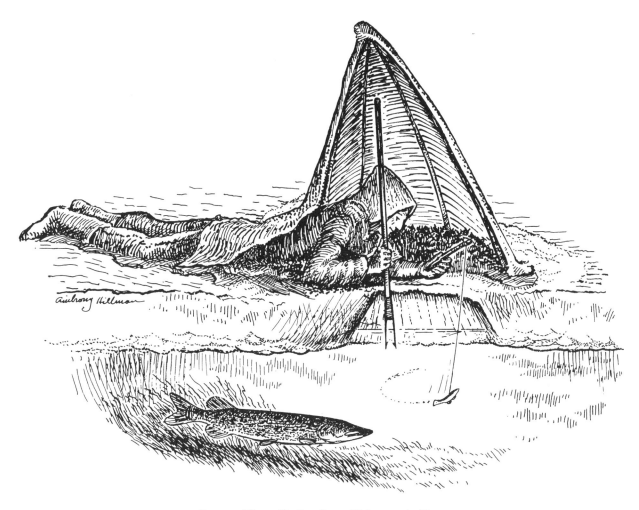

Cutaway View of Indian Spear Fisherman in Tent

# Introduction: The Spear Fisherman and the Decoy

Ages before the white man came to North America, Indian and Inuit (Eskimo) peoples of the frozen North were catching fish by spearing them. In the deepest part of winter, when most inland waters were covered with thick ice, the spear fisherman would cut a hole in the ice, its sides opening out to afford a wider angle of view. He would then erect a small tent over the hole by wrapping skins (in later years, blankets) around a framework of saplings. Loose snow packed around the tent kept stray rays of light from peeping under it and betraying the fisherman who lay patiently in wait with his spear. The only light by which he could see his prey was the eerie, unworldly glow reflected from the bottom of the lake.

Wasn't this fitting? The spear fisherman lowered into the water a lure that was a little image of a fish he had carved, with religious devotion and patience, in bone or ivory. He had prayed to the Fish Spirit that his lure would be acceptable and the thrust of his spear true. Everything had been prepared with

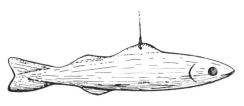

Inuit "Fish" of Ivory

utmost care. The decoy was attached by several feet of line to a small jigging stick, and he had even carved gills and scales into the carefully shaped little model. Soon a large, swift and powerful fish would come to devour the magical lure that he had fashioned by his own hands and ingenuity, with the help of the Fish Spirit. He was patient, his barbed spear point ready.

And so it went for hundreds of years. Then the white man came to the North and was inspired to fish with spear and decoy in a similar manner. A tradition of fish-decoy carving developed with the white man too, although his carvings were more often of wood and metal, and were weighted with lead. They were of many different styles, some very realistic representations of bait fish or of other fish, found in local waters, that were typically the object of the anglers' efforts.

The 17 decoys (actually 19, counting the smallmouth bass and the alternate version of the yellow perch) that you can make from the patterns and instructions in this book are, in their specifics, of my own design. They, however, incorporate many features and in general follow the tradition, in all its amazing variety, of the early white settlers who in their time had followed that of the Indians and Eskimos. All of the fish these carvings represent are well-known northern North American species once commonly portrayed in decoys intended for use in spear fishing. In some regions the age-old sport of spear fishing on the ice with hand-carved decoys continues today.

# How to Use This Book

This is a pattern book. It gets cut up as a matter of course. But before you cut it to pieces, *read the instructions!* Here are some general tips to keep in mind as you proceed.

## Wood

First, about the selection of wood. Basswood, or linden, is excellent for carving fish decoys and is traditionally used for this purpose in the Great Lakes region. It is a fine-grained wood that takes detail well if you want to get fancy. Basswood is fairly plentiful today and its use does not contribute to the decimation of tropical forests or Southern United States wetlands. White pine and sugar pine are also fine traditional carving woods. Walnut was used by a number of carvers to provide a beautiful natural finish. Cedar is also suitable, but the tails of the carvings must be left thicker when using this soft wood. Explore what is available from sawmills in your area. Even a small amount of scrap construction lumber can yield enough wood to keep you busy for many winter nights.

I have indicated the dimensions of the wood stock necessary for each carving; these measurements are a little large, to facilitate sawing out the basic shape around the template (it is always easier when the blade of the saw can make one smoothly flowing, continuous cut).

## Fins

Fins for fish decoys with wooden bodies are usually made of sheet metal. Metal fins have great advantages over wood: they are strong, can be cut without worrying about grain direction and can be painted or polished as desired.

Tin snips work well for cutting out the fin shapes used in this book. I prefer copper roof-flashing material for most applications, but I used aluminum for a few carvings where a silver color was desired. Also suitable for fins is the metal from tin cans, as long as it is stiff enough. Cut the can apart and hammer the metal flat. With any of these metals, fine details, such as those on the walleye or bluegill fins, may be added with an assortment of files.

Another option is to avoid cutting out fins at all by using prestamped spinner blades that are a component of fishing lures. The range of sizes available covers almost all the requirements of the patterns in this book. Spinner blades have a curve bent into them; hammer this flat, and insert the "hole end" into the wooden body of the carving.

You may obtain spinner blades from many fishing-tackle supply shops. A good mail-order source that I recommend is Reed Tackle, Box 1250, Marshalls Creek, PA 18335. It is a good idea to telephone for information first: (717) 223-7044. This supplier has a knowledgeable staff and ships promptly. Spinner blades are generally purchased by the dozen or the hundred. They come in nickel, brass and copper finishes, and sizes vary from #00 ($^7/_{16}$") to #6 ($1^7/_8$"), depending on the shape and style.

Securing metal fins to the body of the decoy is a prime consideration. If your carving is weighted with lead, you can set the fins into the lead cavity before pouring in the molten lead. Dorsal fins with holes used as line ties should be drilled and pinned to the body for permanence. I also use "super glue" for additional bonding. Fins can also be screwed into the body after predrilling.

## Tails

The tails of fish decoys are usually made of wood and are not carved separately from the main piece. Leather was a popular material for decoy tails in the Lake Chatauqua area of New York State. When using a tail of leather or metal, use brads or brass pins to secure it to the body. On a metal tail, rays may be simulated with an electric metal engraving tool. Similarly, with a wooden tail, rays may be formed with a gouge (my preference) or wood-burned. If you have carved the tail a bit thin, use "super glue" to saturate the cells of the wood, as this will substantially strengthen the fragile parts.

## Line Ties

All fish decoys require line ties, and several variations are commonly employed. On some carvings, such as those of the bass and bluegill, the dorsal fin can be drilled, as mentioned above, and pinned securely to the body. A multiple wire tie, such as the one shown on the redhorse, was frequently used. Indian and Inuit "primitive" decoys were often drilled through the body and a line was secured through this hole. When using a screw eye, as on the brook-trout decoy, make a small pilot hole and coat the threads with epoxy before inserting the screw eye into the body. On traditional fish decoys every and any type of fastener available was used. I find brass and copper to be excellent because of their resistance to corrosion as well as being easy to hammer, drill and shape.

## Eyes

A word about eyes. For a "folksy" approach, eyes of decoys may be carved and painted, or you may even wish to try tacks, glass beads, rhinestones, etc. On more realistic carvings, glass eyes look best. Clear eyes on wire may be purchased and painted (on the *back* of each eye) as required, or you may wish to buy premium eyes made especially to represent specific species. The Tohickon Glass Eye Company (Erwinna, PA 18920) manufactures some of the finest glass eyes available for fish carvings. With each set of patterns I have provided information about the size and color of the eyes (eyes are of glass unless specifically noted otherwise).

## Weighting

Spear fishing is now legal in only a few states. If you are permitted to spear fish and wish to use any of these carvings as real decoys, it will be necessary to weight your carving with lead. If your carvings are intended for decorative purposes only, you may skip this procedure.

My method requires using an electric melting pot. It is easier and safer than other methods, and most fishing-tackle shops can supply a melting pot—they are used in making lead sinkers.

CAUTION: Before you work with lead, there are certain things you should be aware of and certain procedures to follow. Lead is toxic and should not be handled without gloves; I recommend burn-proof gloves. The fumes from molten lead can make you ill; wear eye protection and work in a well-ventilated area. Do not melt lead in the typically confined area of a kitchen. The fumes can poison food, and a pot full of molten lead is a hazard to anyone passing through.

*(Instructions continue after Plates.)*

# Brown Trout *(Salmo trutta)*

*A native of the Old World, introduced to this continent about a hundred years ago.*

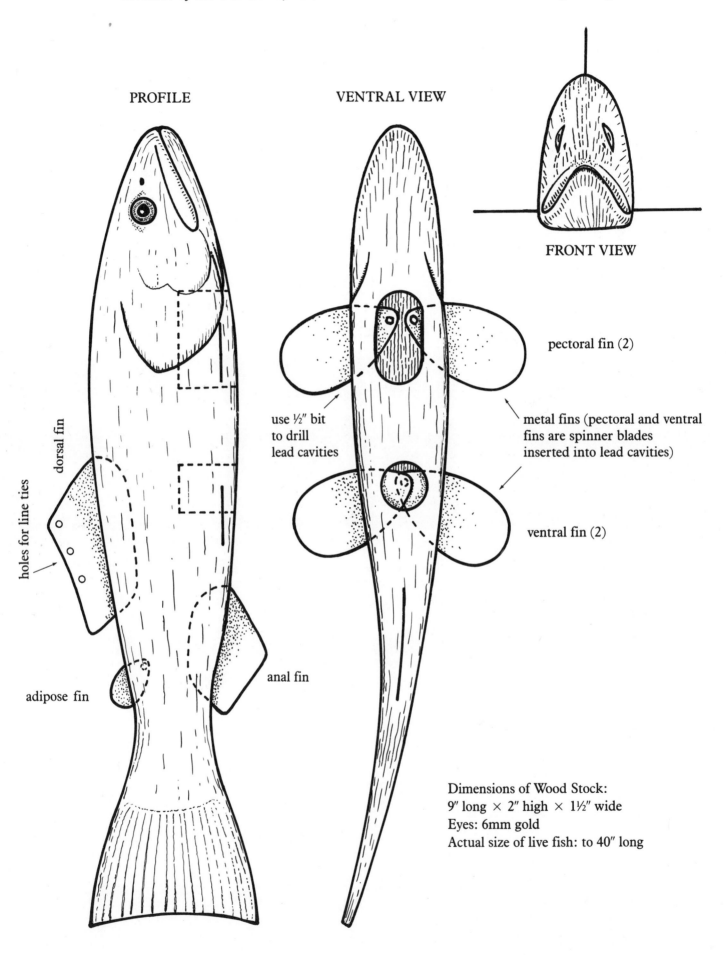

PROFILE

VENTRAL VIEW

FRONT VIEW

pectoral fin (2)

metal fins (pectoral and ventral fins are spinner blades inserted into lead cavities)

ventral fin (2)

use ½″ bit to drill lead cavities

dorsal fin

holes for line ties

adipose fin

anal fin

Dimensions of Wood Stock:
9″ long × 2″ high × 1½″ wide
Eyes: 6mm gold
Actual size of live fish: to 40″ long

Plate 1 (left)

*Remove staples to see and use full patterns.*

# Largemouth Bass *(Micropterus salmoides)*

### (with head detail of Smallmouth Bass, *M. dolomieui*)

*Largemouth and smallmouth basses are among the most sought-after game fishes in North America. Sunfish family.*

FRONT VIEW

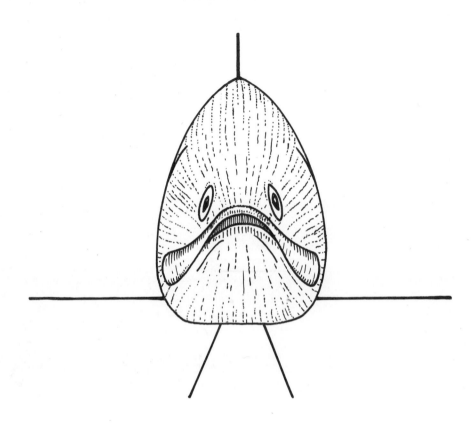

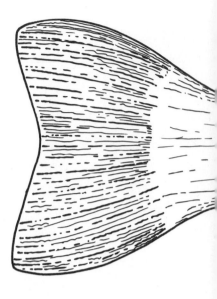

saw edge to center of eye

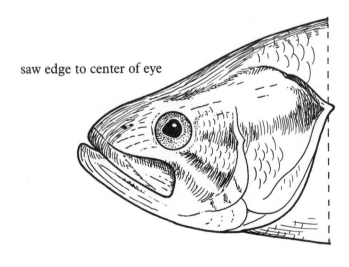

HEAD OF SMALLMOUTH BASS
(cut out and glue to largemouth
head on blank side of template)

Plate 2 (left)

*Remove staples to see and use full patterns.*

# Yellow Perch *(Perca flavescens)*

*A schooling fish, popular with anglers, that moves from deeper*
*to shallower water to feed early and late in the day.*

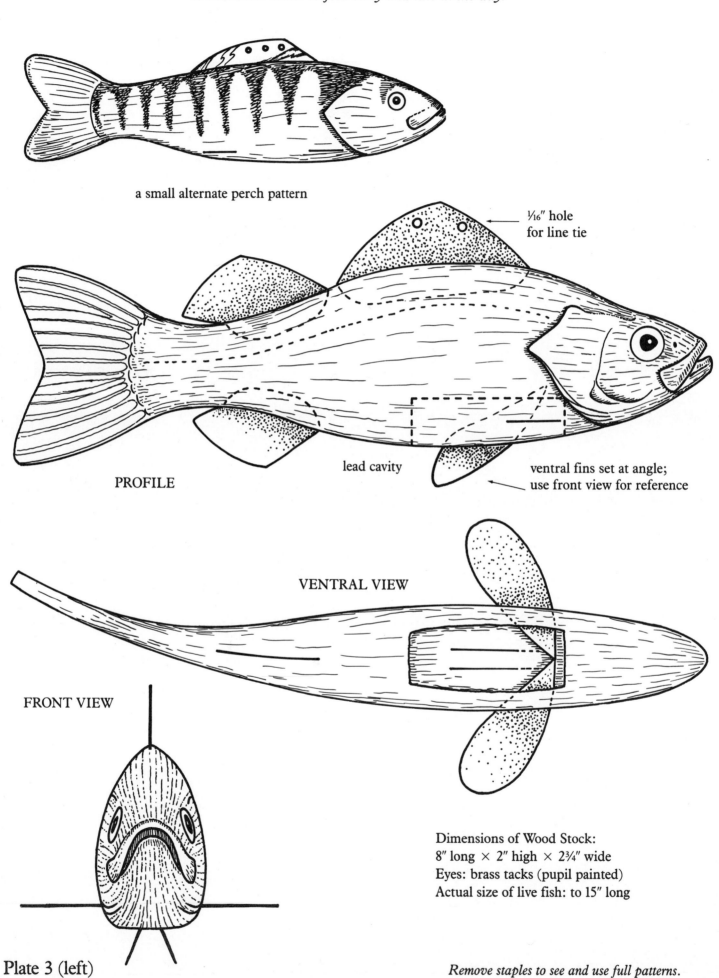

a small alternate perch pattern

¹⁄₁₆″ hole
for line tie

PROFILE

lead cavity

ventral fins set at angle;
use front view for reference

VENTRAL VIEW

FRONT VIEW

Dimensions of Wood Stock:
8″ long × 2″ high × 2¾″ wide
Eyes: brass tacks (pupil painted)
Actual size of live fish: to 15″ long

Plate 3 (left)

*Remove staples to see and use full patterns.*

PROFILE

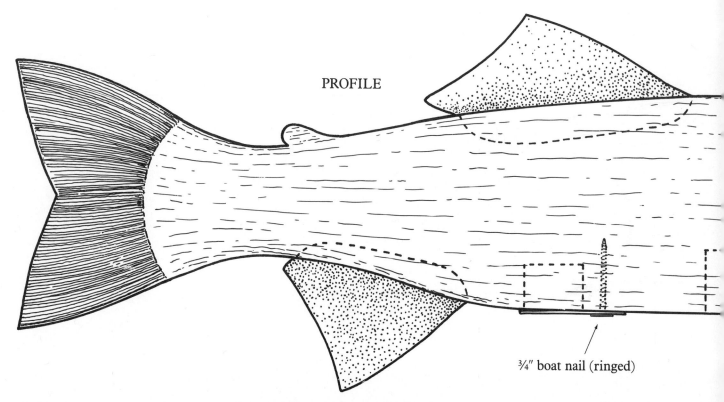

¾″ boat nail (ringed)

fins cut from sheet copper roof flashing

Dimensions of Wood Stock:
12½″ long × 3″ high × 2¼″ wide
Eyes: 11mm pale gold
Actual size of live fish: to 45″ long

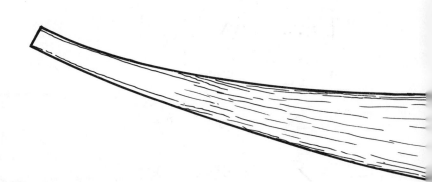

# Rainbow Trout *(Salmo gairdneri)*

*One of the best-looking—and -tasting—of the trouts. Like their relatives the salmon,
some rainbow trout live part of their lives in the ocean before returning to fresh water to breed.*

Plate 4 (left)

*Remove staples to see and use full patterns.*

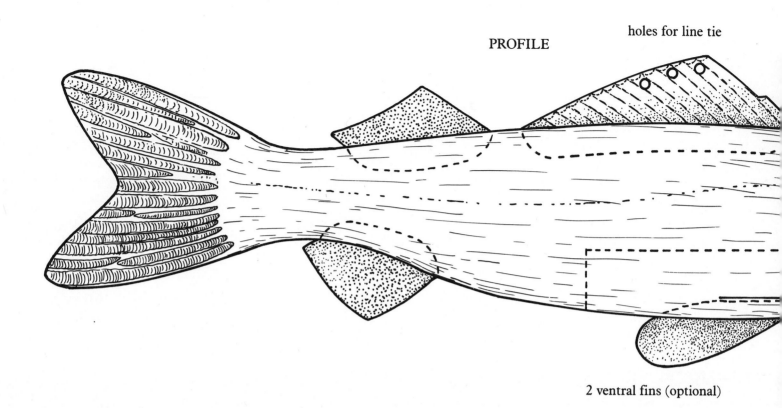

PROFILE

holes for line tie

2 ventral fins (optional)

fins cut from sheet copper roof flashing

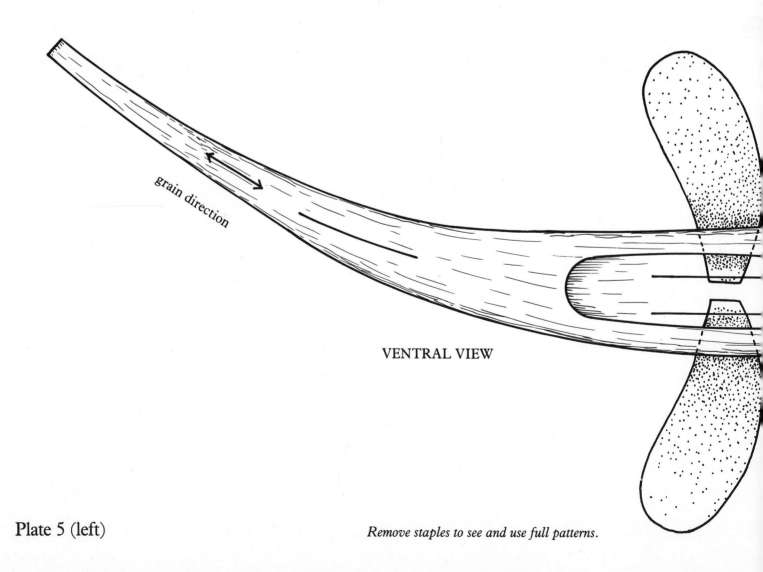

grain direction

VENTRAL VIEW

Plate 5 (left)

*Remove staples to see and use full patterns.*

# River Redhorse *(Moxostoma carinatum)*

*This member of the sucker family, as the family name suggests, sucks up its food from river bottoms.*

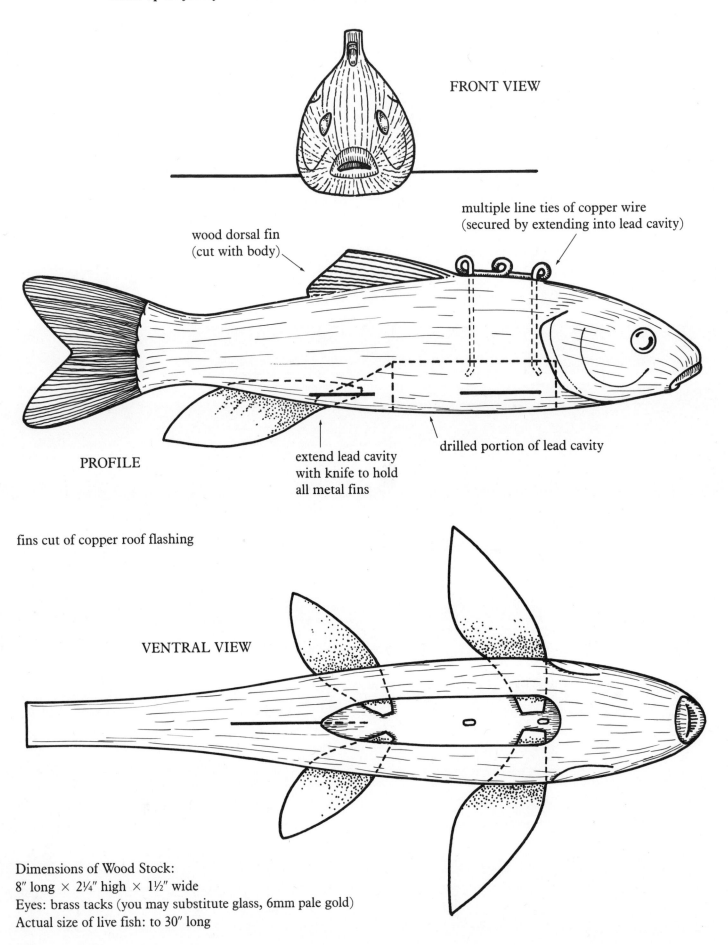

FRONT VIEW

multiple line ties of copper wire
(secured by extending into lead cavity)

wood dorsal fin
(cut with body)

drilled portion of lead cavity

PROFILE

extend lead cavity
with knife to hold
all metal fins

fins cut of copper roof flashing

VENTRAL VIEW

Dimensions of Wood Stock:
8″ long × 2¼″ high × 1½″ wide
Eyes: brass tacks (you may substitute glass, 6mm pale gold)
Actual size of live fish: to 30″ long

Plate 6 (left)

*Remove staples to see and use full patterns.*

# Bluegill *(Lepomis macrochirus)*

*The most common of all members of the sunfish family.*

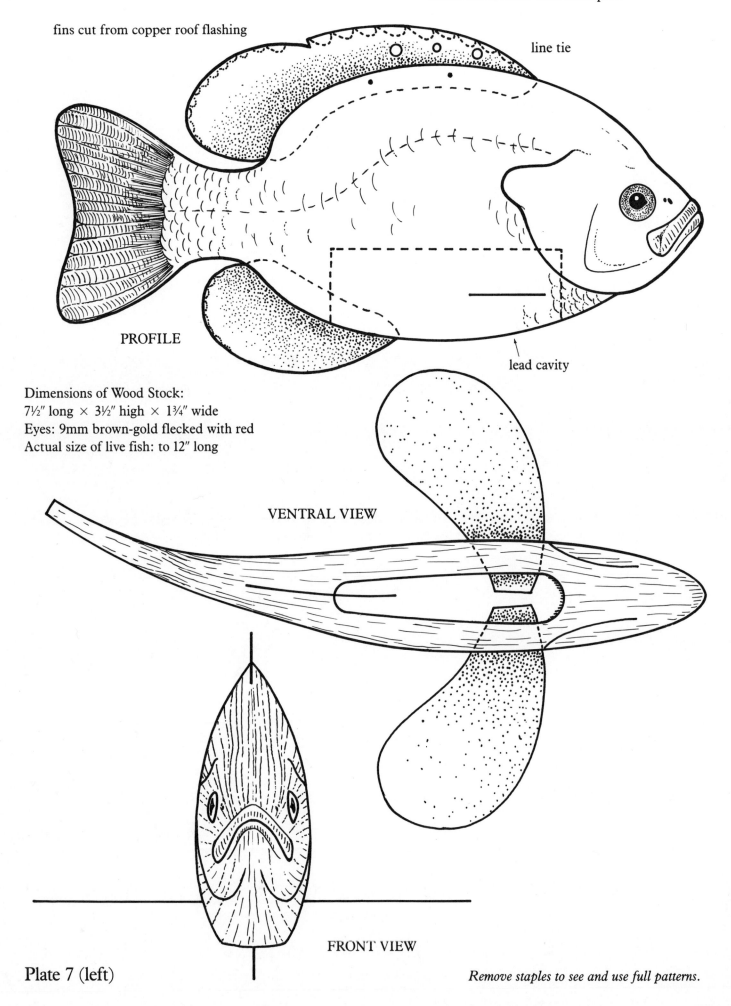

dorsal fin secured with brass pins

fins cut from copper roof flashing

line tie

PROFILE

lead cavity

Dimensions of Wood Stock:
7½″ long × 3½″ high × 1¾″ wide
Eyes: 9mm brown-gold flecked with red
Actual size of live fish: to 12″ long

VENTRAL VIEW

FRONT VIEW

Plate 7 (left)

*Remove staples to see and use full patterns.*

# Northern Pike *(Esox lucius)*

*Found throughout much of the world, this large predatory fish
is very popular with North American fishermen.*

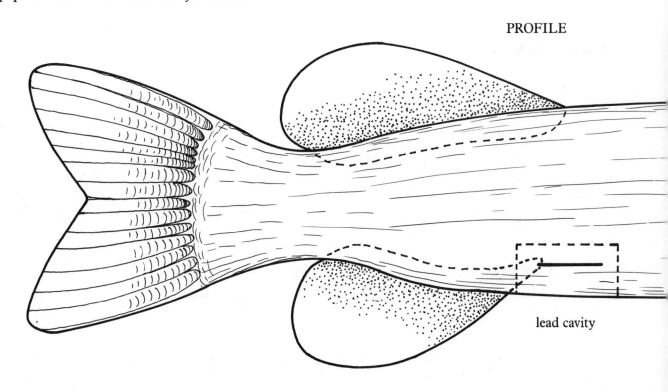

lead cavity

Dimensions of Wood Stock:
15″ long × 3½″ high × 2″ wide
Eyes: 9mm silver-brown and gold
Actual size of live fish: to 52″ long

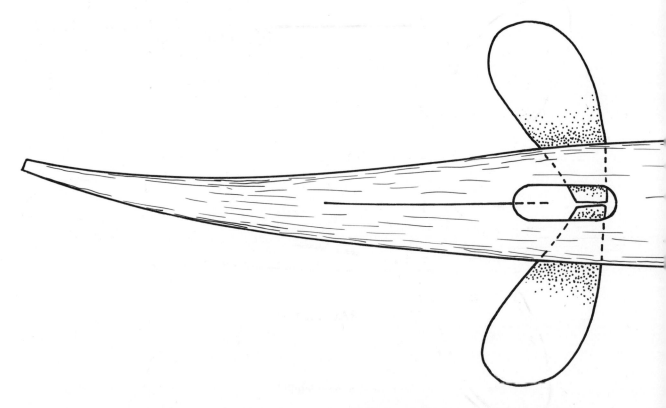

Plate 8 (left)

*Remove staples to see and use full patterns.*

# Round Whitefish *(Prosopium cylindraceum)*

*Good eating, but less common than its cousin the lake whitefish. Trout family.*

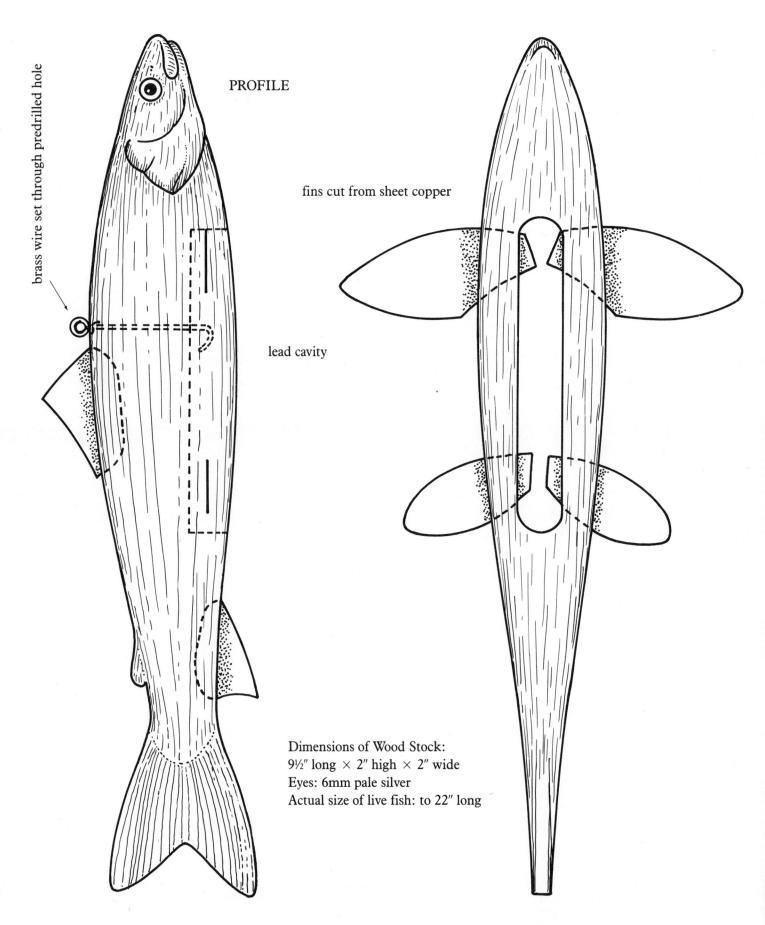

PROFILE

brass wire set through predrilled hole

fins cut from sheet copper

lead cavity

Dimensions of Wood Stock:
9½″ long × 2″ high × 2″ wide
Eyes: 6mm pale silver
Actual size of live fish: to 22″ long

VENTRAL VIEW

Plate 9 (left)

*Remove staples to see and use full patterns.*

PROFILE

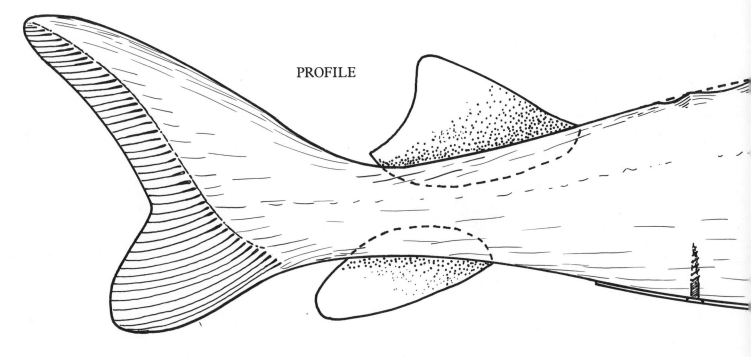

fins cut from sheet metal, secured with four ½″ flathead screws
(front screws drilled into lead, or pour lead around screws)

VENTRAL VIEW

FRONT VIEW

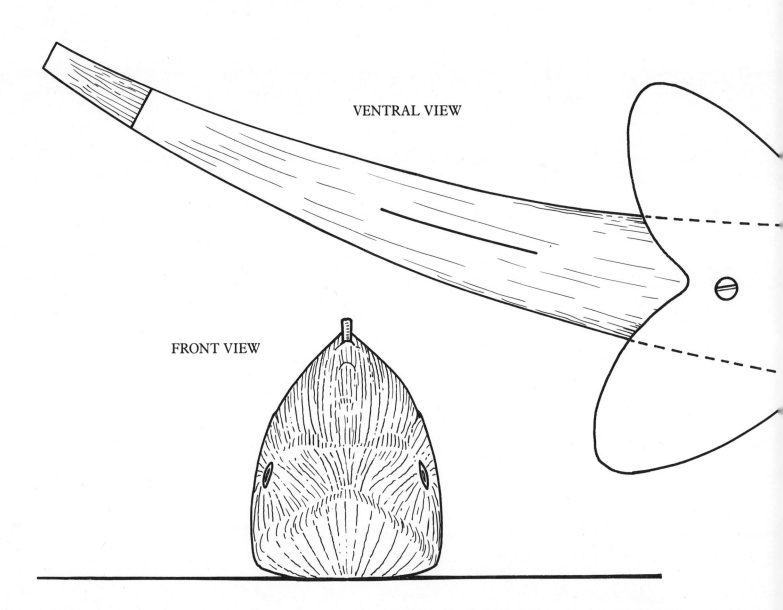

Plate 10 (left)

*Remove staples to see and use full patterns.*

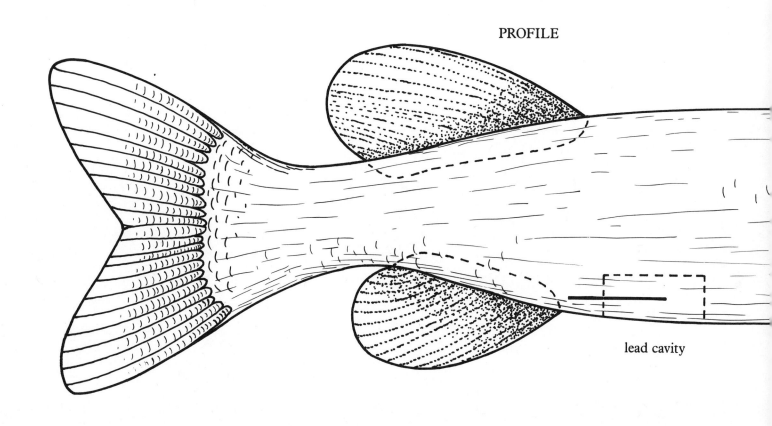

lead cavity

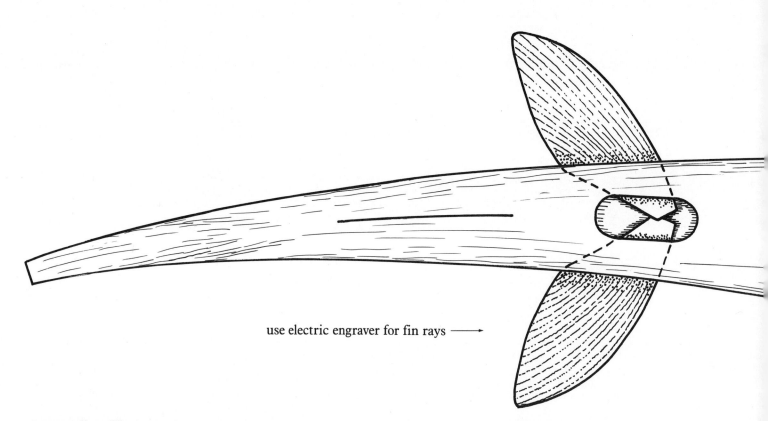

use electric engraver for fin rays ⟶

# Muskellunge *(Esox masquinongy)* (swallowing yellow perch)

*This largest pike is the fiercest predator of them all, and the most favored by anglers.*

Plate 11 (left)

*Remove staples to see and use full patterns.*

PROFILE

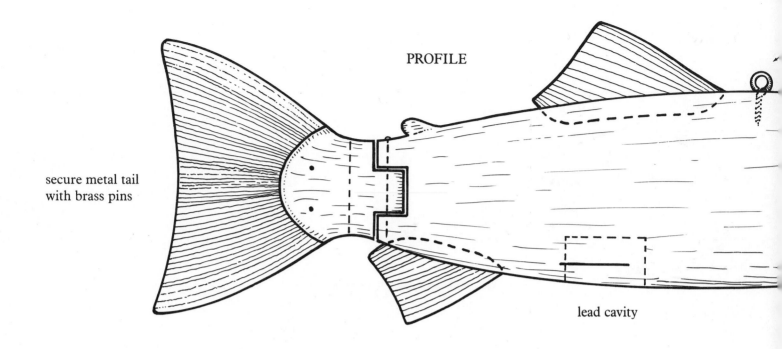

secure metal tail
with brass pins

lead cavity

cut hinged body pieces separately; finish, seal and
prime hinged parts before joining (alternatively,
use jigsaw to cut entire body as one piece)

all fins, including tail, cut from aluminum roof flashing

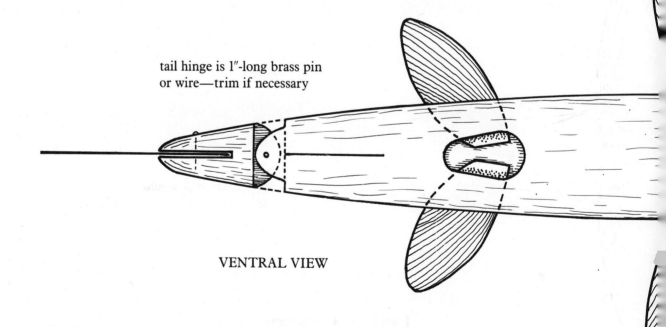

tail hinge is 1″-long brass pin
or wire—trim if necessary

VENTRAL VIEW

Plate 12 (left)

*Remove staples to see and use full patterns.*

line tie is screw eye
set with epoxy

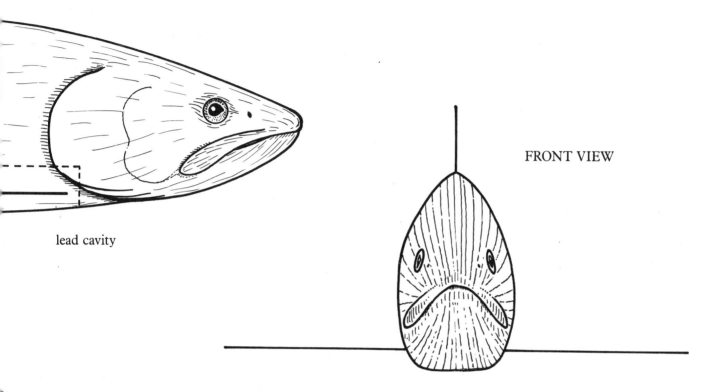

lead cavity

FRONT VIEW

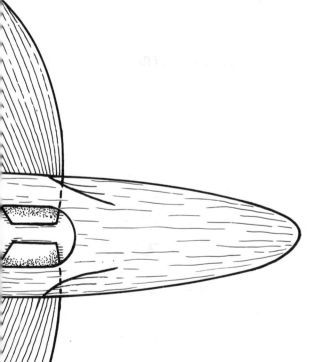

Dimensions of Wood Stock:
9½″ long × 2½″ high × 1¾″ wide
Eyes: 6mm yellow-gold
Actual size of live fish: to 39″ long

# Coho Salmon *(Oncorhynchus kisutch)*

*Because this Pacific Coast salmon is a vigorous fighter when hooked and makes great eating, it is a real prize to fishermen.*

*Remove staples to see and use full patterns.*

Plate 12 (right)

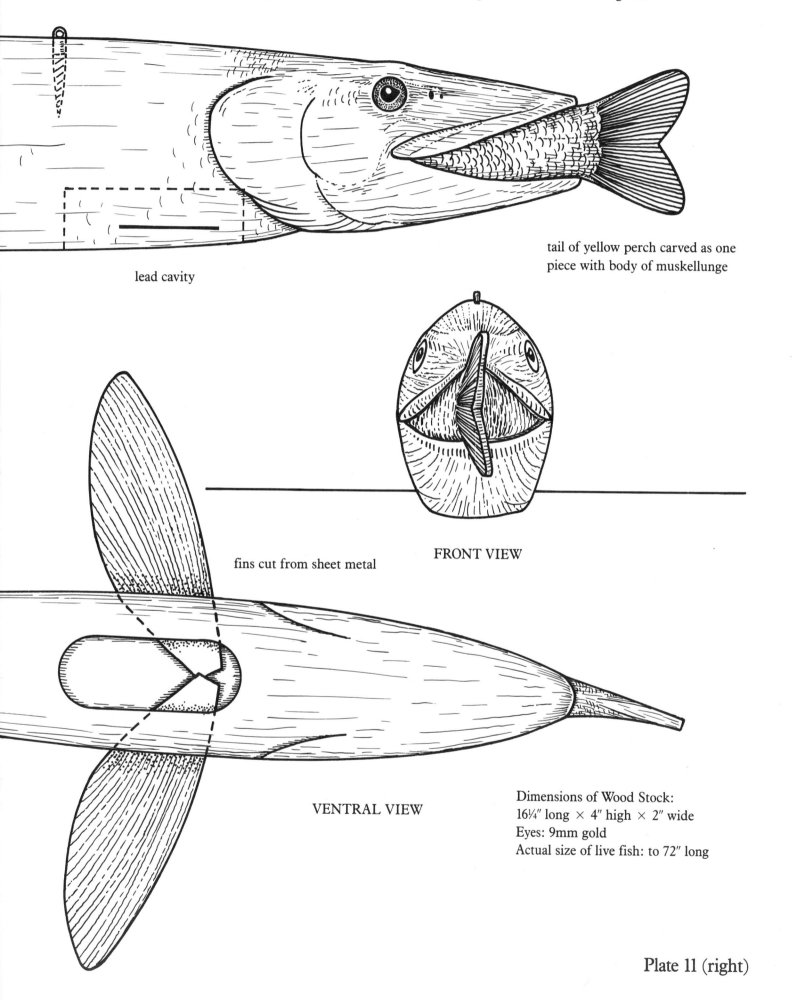

line tie made from 1″ brass screw; saw head off,
pound shaft flat and drill with ¹⁄₁₆″ bit;
predrill hole and set screw with epoxy

after body and head (with perch tail) are sanded
smooth, relief-cut jaws; then cut-in fin rays
and scales of perch with wood-burning tool

lead cavity

tail of yellow perch carved as one
piece with body of muskellunge

fins cut from sheet metal

FRONT VIEW

VENTRAL VIEW

Dimensions of Wood Stock:
16¼″ long × 4″ high × 2″ wide
Eyes: 9mm gold
Actual size of live fish: to 72″ long

Plate 11 (right)

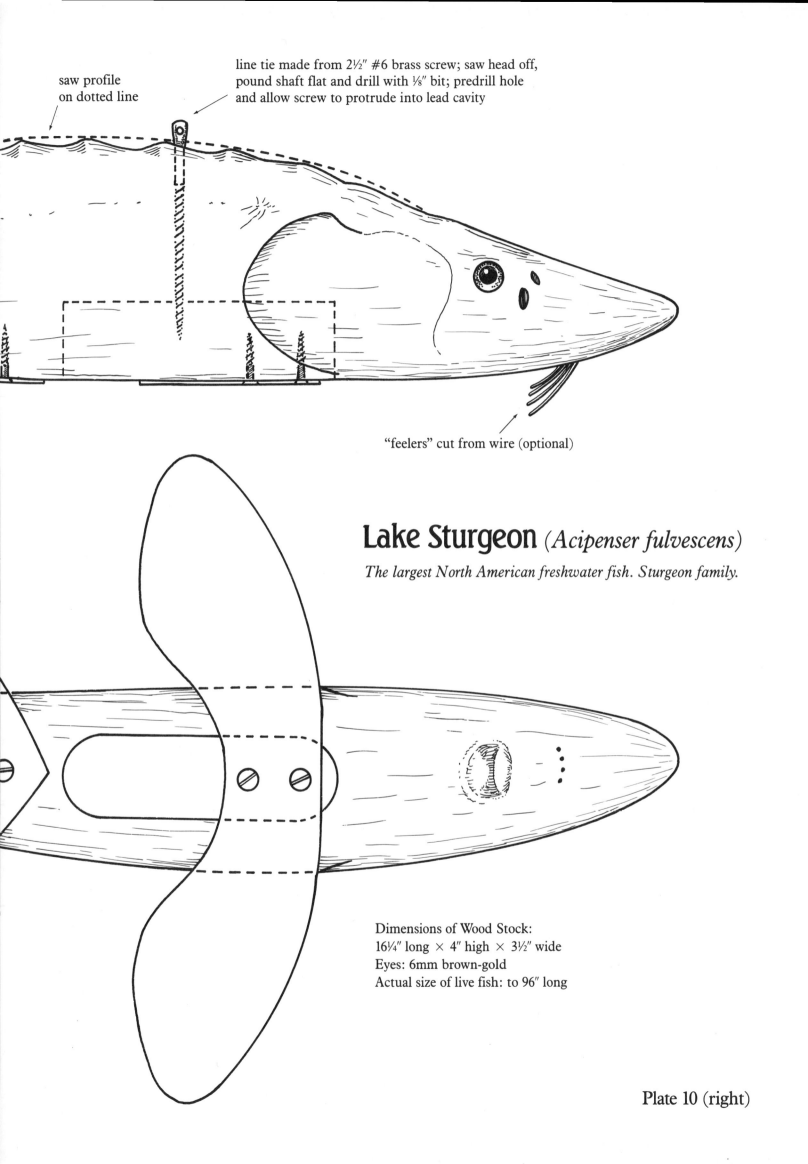

saw profile
on dotted line

line tie made from 2½″ #6 brass screw; saw head off,
pound shaft flat and drill with ⅛″ bit; predrill hole
and allow screw to protrude into lead cavity

"feelers" cut from wire (optional)

# Lake Sturgeon *(Acipenser fulvescens)*

*The largest North American freshwater fish. Sturgeon family.*

Dimensions of Wood Stock:
16¼″ long × 4″ high × 3½″ wide
Eyes: 6mm brown-gold
Actual size of live fish: to 96″ long

Plate 10 (right)

# Lake Whitefish *(Coregonus clupeaformis)*

*An important commercial fish in the trout family. Excellent eating.*

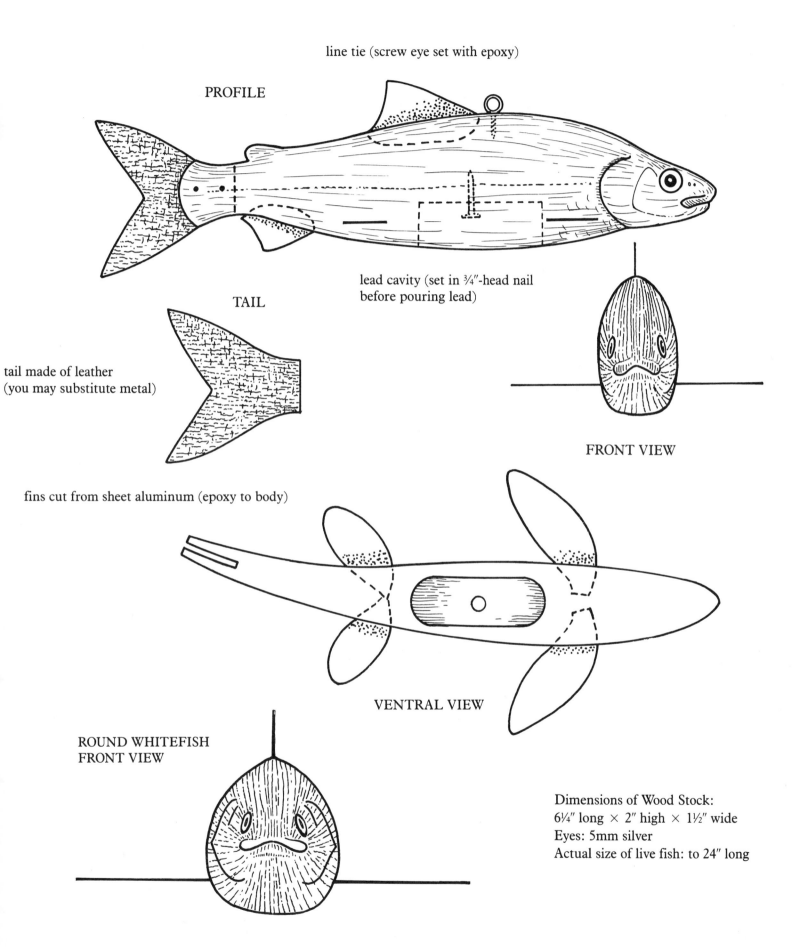

line tie (screw eye set with epoxy)

PROFILE

lead cavity (set in ¾″-head nail
before pouring lead)

TAIL

tail made of leather
(you may substitute metal)

FRONT VIEW

fins cut from sheet aluminum (epoxy to body)

VENTRAL VIEW

ROUND WHITEFISH
FRONT VIEW

Dimensions of Wood Stock:
6¼″ long × 2″ high × 1½″ wide
Eyes: 5mm silver
Actual size of live fish: to 24″ long

*Remove staples to see and use full patterns.*

Plate 9 (right)

line tie enters lead cavity

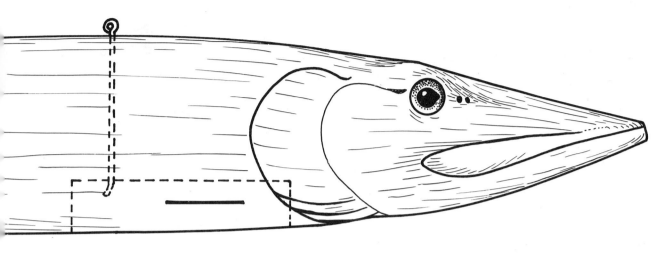

lead cavity

FRONT VIEW

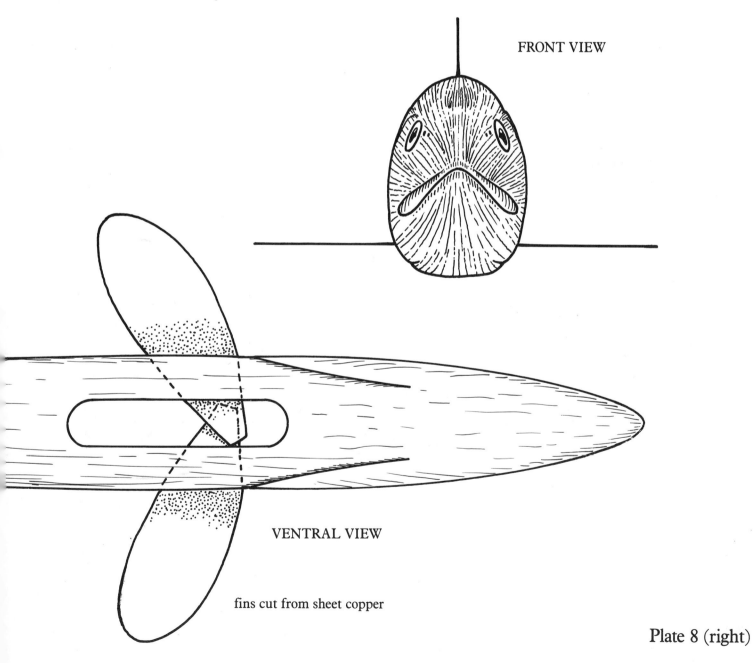

VENTRAL VIEW

fins cut from sheet copper

Plate 8 (right)

# Black Crappie *(Pomoxis nigromaculatus)*

*Popular with anglers in the deep South as well as the North. Sunfish family.*

FRONT VIEW

Dimensions of Wood Stock:
7″ long × 3½″ high × 1½″ wide
Eyes: 9mm brown-gold flecked with vertical black bar
Actual size of live fish: to 16″ long

wood dorsal fin, cut out with body
(if aluminum or other metal fin substituted,
use dotted line as guide)

line tie is brass screw
eye set with epoxy

tail rays cut
with gouge

lead cavity

anal fin of
sheet aluminum

PROFILE

pectoral fins made of Colorado #4
spoon blades, pounded flat

VENTRAL VIEW

Plate 5 (recto)

# Cisco *(Coregonus artedii)*

*A small relative of trout, salmon and whitefish.*

PROFILE

drill holes through body and tail,
secure with brass pins

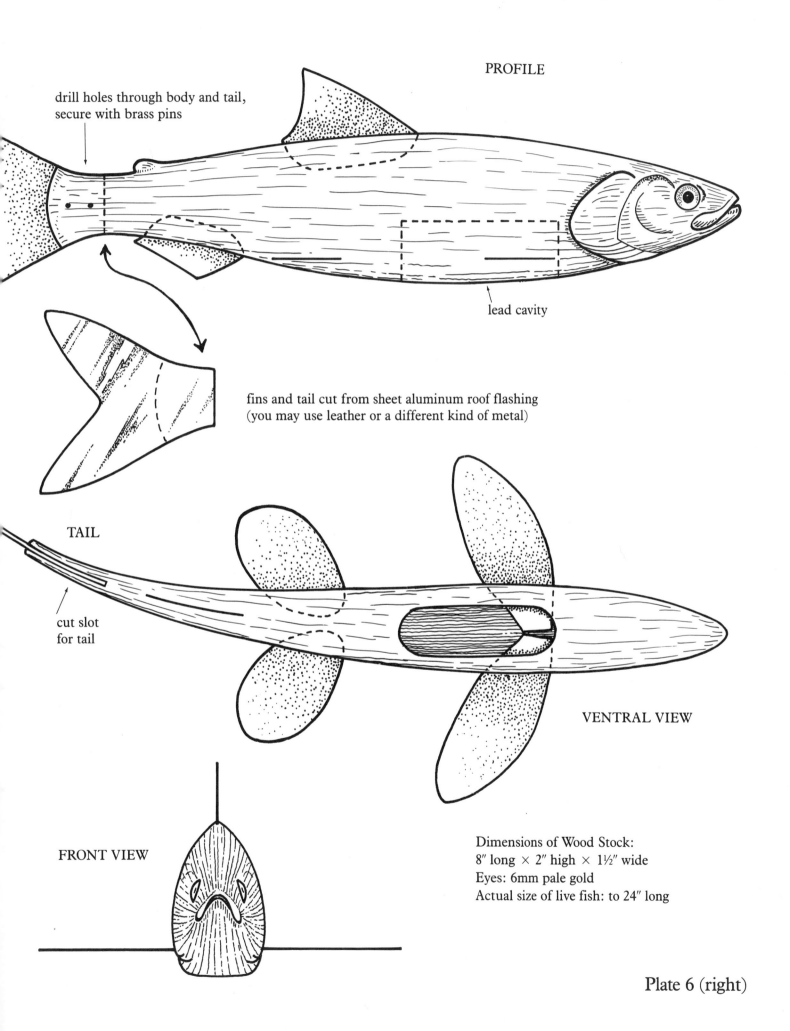

lead cavity

fins and tail cut from sheet aluminum roof flashing
(you may use leather or a different kind of metal)

TAIL

cut slot
for tail

VENTRAL VIEW

FRONT VIEW

Dimensions of Wood Stock:
8″ long × 2″ high × 1½″ wide
Eyes: 6mm pale gold
Actual size of live fish: to 24″ long

Plate 6 (right)

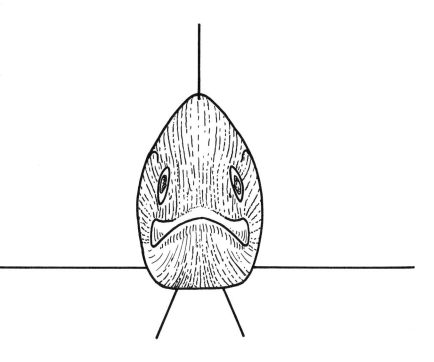

FRONT VIEW

Dimensions of Wood Stock:
11½″ long × 2¾″ high × 4½″ wide
   (experienced carvers may use 2¼″-wide
   piece, allowing grain to run diagonally
   across tail)
Eyes: 10mm special walleye type
Actual size of live fish: to 41″ long

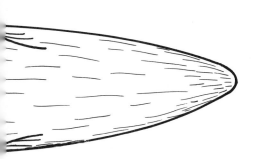

# Walleye *(Stizostedion vitreum)*

*The walleyed "pike," as this popular fish is often known among
anglers, is really the largest member of the perch family.*

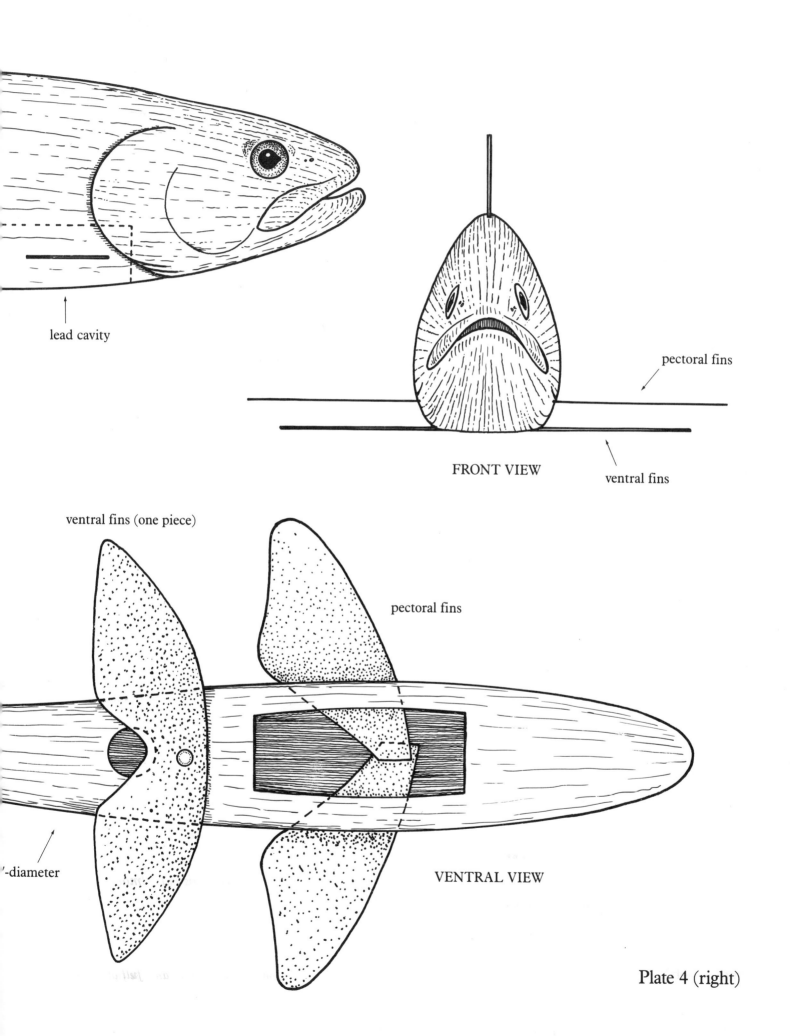

lead cavity

pectoral fins

FRONT VIEW

ventral fins

ventral fins (one piece)

pectoral fins

-diameter

VENTRAL VIEW

Plate 4 (right)

# Golden Shiner *(Notemigonus crysoleucas)*

*This relative of the carps and minnows is commonly used as a bait fish.*

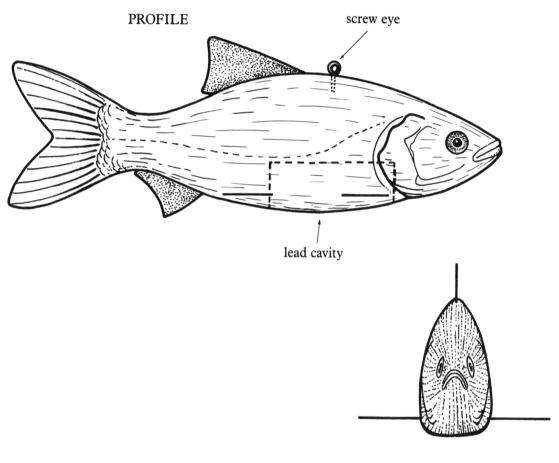

PROFILE

screw eye

lead cavity

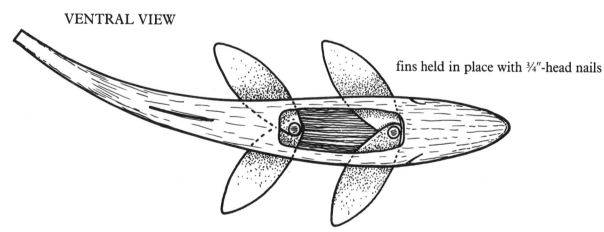

FRONT VIEW

VENTRAL VIEW

fins held in place with ¾"-head nails

Dimensions of Wood Stock:
5¾" long × 2¼" high × 1½" wide
Eyes: 6mm gold (painted on)
Actual size of live fish: to 12" long

use sheet copper for dorsal and anal fins (2), "willow"-pattern
spinner blades for pectoral and ventral fins (4)

PROFILE

line ties (holes approx. 1/16″)

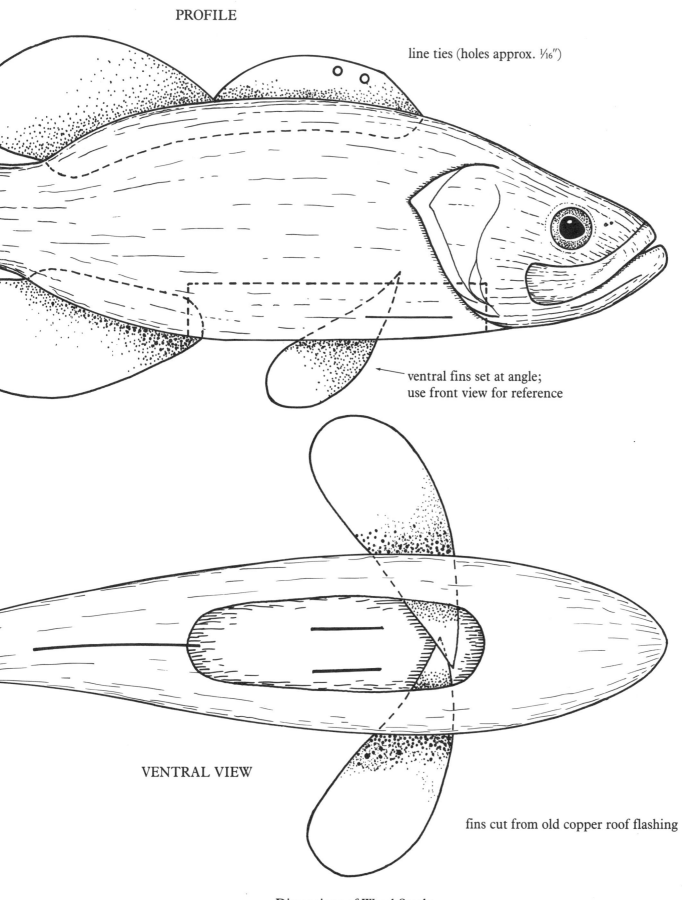

ventral fins set at angle;
use front view for reference

VENTRAL VIEW

fins cut from old copper roof flashing

Dimensions of Wood Stock:
10¾″ long × 3½″ high × 2¾″ wide
Eyes: 11mm brown-gold
Actual size of live fish: to 38″ long
   (smallmouth bass: to 24″)

*Remove staples to see and use full patterns.*

Plate 2 (right)

# Brook Trout *(Salvelinus fontinalis)*

*A colorful, popular game fish.*

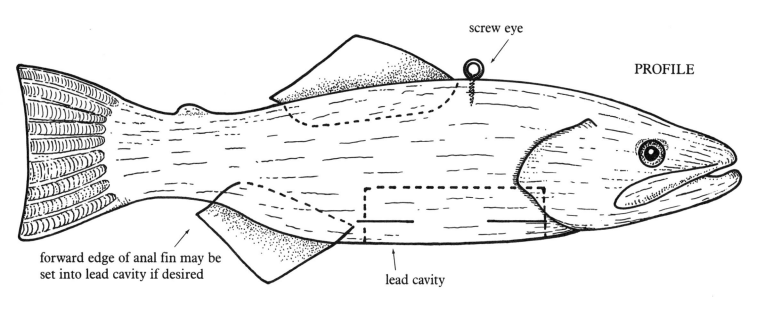

screw eye

PROFILE

forward edge of anal fin may be
set into lead cavity if desired

lead cavity

fins cut from old copper roof flashing

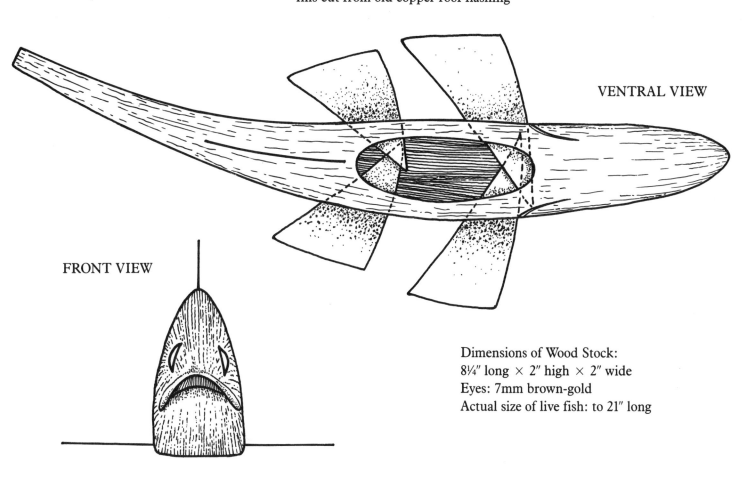

VENTRAL VIEW

FRONT VIEW

Dimensions of Wood Stock:
8¼″ long × 2″ high × 2″ wide
Eyes: 7mm brown-gold
Actual size of live fish: to 21″ long

*Remove staples to see and use full patterns.*

Plate 1 (right)

More about the lead-weighting process will be explained in the carving instructions that follow. Just one more comment here. A friend of mine who speared fish in Michigan for some twenty years weighted his decoys (up to eight inches long) with split lead shot and Duco Cement™! It worked fine, and he didn't have to worry about the hazards of fire and hot lead. My point is that, as you gain experience in carving, you should feel free to experiment. You may come up with a modification of the traditional methods that no one else ever thought of, yet is just right for your purposes.

Before you begin, read through the general instructions. Remove the staples from the book and spread the pages out flat. Decide which decoy you would like to carve. Read any specific instructions on the Plates describing special procedures for that carving. A #11 X-ACTO knife is excellent for cutting out the patterns. Go to it and have fun: that's what it's all about.

# Instructions

## Carving the Head, Body and Tail

You will notice that profile, ventral (bottom-view) and front-view patterns are provided for each decoy. In some cases you will also find an alternate pattern for the head or tail (in the case of the yellow perch, for the entire fish). Again I remind you to read carefully any special intructions that appear with the patterns for the decoy of your choice before beginning.

When you are confident that you understand the general procedures for, and any special characteristics of, the decoy you have chosen to carve, you may begin. Carefully cut out the complete ventral (bottom) pattern and the profile pattern. These will be the main templates used directly to cut out the shape from the wood. Be very careful to include the fins on both templates (those typically found on the profile template are illustrated in Figure 1). There will usually be a dorsal and an anal fin, and a pair each of pectoral and ventral fins. Trout and other salmonids, as well as some other fishes, also have a small adipose (fleshy) fin near the tail.

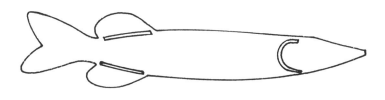

Fig. 1. Gill Slit and Slits for Cutting Out Fins

For most decoys, you will now need to cut out a set of fins. Cut slits in the profile template as shown in Fig. 1 (the slit on the right is for tracing the gill covers). Now trace the outlines of the fins onto wood or metal of suitable dimensions (be sure that there is plenty of extra material to facilitate easy sawing) and saw them out. Similarly trace and cut out any fins you need that are shown on the ventral template. Naturally you will skip these steps in any case where a fin is carved out together with the body.

If you are interested primarily in making a working decoy, you should keep in mind that it is important to test a design in the water after you have carved it out and attached the fins. You may find that some modifications of fin design and placement are called for. Be aware that many old fish decoys had a minimum of fins; some had no fins!

The ventral (underside) patterns, besides providing a view of fin placement, indicate the width and curve of the carvings. They are also used to saw out the "top" view; you can have the fish curve in any direction you want by flipping this template over if necessary. Cutting slits between body and fins will, as for the profile template, help you mark the wood for cutting. You will notice that some of the decoys are not curved at all. Such decoys tend to "dart" in the water. If you are creating a working decoy or simply prefer a curve in your decoy for whatever reason, you may use your judgment to add a curve as you saw out the "blank" (uncarved, sawn-out shape). With practice, as you become accustomed to the dimensions of a particular type of decoy, you will be able to do this without even using a ventral template. In any case, leave plenty of extra wood at the head and tail ends, sawing up to the ends of the block of wood (see Fig. 2).

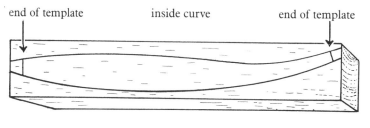

end of template     inside curve     end of template

outside curve

Fig. 2. Wood Marked for Sawing Out Ventral View. Extend Cuts Past Template to Edges of Wood

Usually ¼″ on each end is satisfactory. Be careful also to leave plenty of extra wood in the part that will become the tail. Sawing it extra-thick will do no harm, but if you saw it too thin the tail may become very fragile as you carve it down to its final size. This can become a serious problem if you are using a soft wood, such as cedar or pine. Also be careful not to cut the wood so the grain runs at a sharp angle to the length of the tail.

Now take the profile template and use an ordinary lead pencil to trace the outline of the profile onto the blank you just sawed out. If the blank is curved, always trace the profile pattern onto the *inside* of the curve (see Fig. 3). Again, make sure that, as far as possible, the grain runs *with* the length of the tail. Saw out the profile.

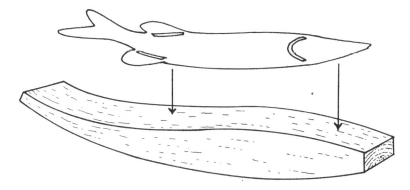

Fig. 3. Trace Template onto Inside Curve. Outside Curve Must Rest on Table when Sawing Out Blank

Next, measure the exact center of the thickness of the blank (from one side of the fish to the other), and draw a centerline completely around the piece (see Fig. 4). Do not cut this guideline away, or you may ruin the symmetry of your carving. It will also help you place the fins properly. The centerline should remain until you give the body its final sanding.

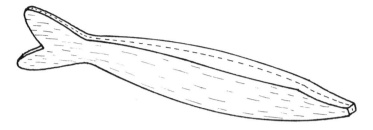

*Fig. 4.* Sawn-Out Blank (Pike) with Centerline

Before you begin to cut away any wood, it is important to understand the final shape you want to arrive at. Study the patterns. You should supplement these with any reference material you can find, including drawings and photographs. Obviously the best reference is a real fish! Aquariums, tackle shops, taxidermy shops and fish markets are all valuable reference sources. An old mounted specimen can sometimes be a useful guide, but use it only in conjunction with other reference material. The colors of fish tend to fade after death.

Now, using the front-view drawing I have provided, carefully carve "downhill" from the thickest parts of the fish (see Fig. 5). That is, the carving direction should be only from the thickest parts to the thinner parts. Do not try to remove too much wood too fast. You should try to maintain a sleek, smoothly curved surface. If you plan to weight your carving with lead, as was done by many traditional decoy carvers, leave the bottom of the carving fairly flat at this point. Once you have removed the corners of the sawn-out block, and the carving is close to its final dimensions, you should mark out the location of the gill covers and any protruding mouth parts so that enough wood is left to carve in the details. Do not carve details on these parts until you have given your carving its final sanding.

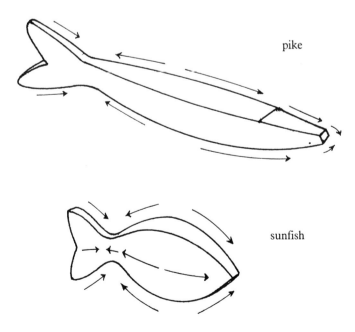

pike

sunfish

*Fig. 5.* Typical Directions for Carving

Be especially careful while carving the tail area! If the carving is curved you will need to cut toward the head from the back edge of the tail—on which side depends on the grain structure (see Fig. 6). You may test the grain by cutting very fine shavings on each side of the tail. Once you have carved the tail down to its proper thickness, you can add detail in a number of ways. I often use a gouge with a shallow sweep (curve); you may prefer to use a burning tool to indicate such details as rays and spines. When, except for these details, the body has been carved as smooth as possible, sand the carving. Begin with coarse sandpaper, then use a medium grit (the cloth-backed type is best), and finish using #220 or finer grit.

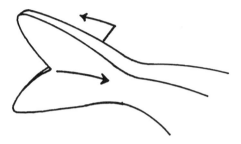

*Fig. 6.* Tail Detail; with Curved Decoys, Cut Toward Head on Inside Curve, Away from Head on Outside Curve

When you are satisfied that the fish from head to tail has been carved and sanded properly, you should next carve or burn in the details of jaws and gill covers. Then, add the eyes. If you are using glass eyes (or other materials for a "folksy" look, as mentioned above), mark their position on the carving and drill holes for them at this time. Be careful not to drill too deep into the heads of fish with highly compressed shapes. Also, be sure that the eyes are in the same place on both sides of the carving or you will create a lopsided look that will ruin everything you have done to this point. Now glue in the eyes.

To carve eyes, make a paper template using as a guide the profile pattern provided here. Marking with a pencil, transfer the shape to the head at the proper location. Cut a line along the pencil mark and then carve to produce a gently rounded eye surface within this scored ring.

Now is the time to add lead weighting to your carving, especially important if you intend to use it as a working decoy. (If your carving is purely for decorative purposes, you may skip this step, but be sure to round out the belly of the fish realistically before sanding.) Turn the fish belly-up and, using the ventral-view pattern as a guide, mark with a pencil the area to be drilled. The centerline should divide this area neatly in half. Now you may proceed to drill out the wood. A drill press with a Forstner bit is the optimum equipment for this operation. If you use a hand-held drill you should clamp the body solidly into a vise so you can control the depth of the cut. Pad the jaws of the vise so as not to crush wood or leave marks. After cutting out the lead cavity, it is a good idea to set a head nail into the body within the cavity. This ensures that the molten lead has something secure to harden around when it cools. This step is less important for those decoys in which the fins protrude into the lead cavity; for other decoys that will be weighted with lead, I strongly advise you not to skip this step.

Next, *before you pour in the molten lead*, you should add the fins. Refer to the special instructions on the Plates and to my general comments on fins, above. The easiest way to cut the slits for the fins (unless you nail or screw them in) is with a small motor-driven cutter, such as a Dremel Moto-Tool™. A ¾"-

diameter steel saw on a ⅛″ shaft (#400) will cut a clean slit about ⁵⁄₁₆″ deep, suitable for most of the decoys in this book. NOTE: To avoid the possibility of serious injury, clamp the decoy securely so that *both* hands are free to hold and guide the tool.

Fin slits may also be cut with a thin-bladed knife and/or a wood-burning tool. Whichever method you use, try fitting the fins into the slits before proceeding with your carving; some adjustments may be in order in either the slits or the fins, or both (see Fig. 7). Note that in most cases the fins (and sometimes the line tie) protrude into the lead cavity. When the fins and any other parts that protrude into the lead cavity are in place, you are ready to pour the lead.

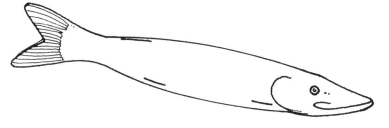

*Fig. 7.* Carving with Fin Slits and Head Detail

It is important to secure the decoy so that the lead sets evenly and level with the edge of the wood. Refer to my earlier comments on lead weighting. Above all, be sure that the lead-pouring operation is done in a *safe* area. Some liquid metal may overflow the top of the cavity. Remember that molten lead is *very* hot, so prepare the surrounding area accordingly. Once the lead has been poured, allow plenty of time for it to cool. Do not touch it *or any metal fins protruding into it* until at least fifteen minutes have elapsed.

## Finishing Your Decoy

After your carving has been given its final sanding, remove all the dust. At this point you may use a wood-burning tool (py-roelectric pen) to burn in scale detail if you wish to make your decoy somewhat realistic. Then you need to consider how you want to finish the carving. Fish decoys may be finished realistically—or as outrageously as you can imagine. It's up to you. Early Indian decoys were often charred to create a dark pattern and sometimes smoked and stained with natural dyes. This method gave the wood a soft and subtle finish. In the last few years, fish decoys have received a lot of attention from collectors, writers and photographers, and hundreds of pictures of old, classic carvings have been published. The range of finishing techniques shown in these pictures is truly mind-boggling.

While, really, anything goes, I have chosen to paint my carvings in a realistic manner, as you can see in the examples shown on the covers of this book. Many of you will want to do the same, and I give here an outline of the procedures to follow.

If you intend to use your carving as an actual working decoy (be aware, however, that spear fishing is legal in only a few states), you need to seal the wood first. The modern carver can choose from a number of different kinds of sealers. I recommend using two coats of sealer. Sand between coats.

Even if your carving is meant only for decorative purposes, you should first coat it with primer. Use a flat white exterior latex (two thin coats are better than one thick one). If you intend to use oil paints, your primer may also be oil-based; latex or acrylic paints require a latex primer. In any case, you should *always use exterior paints* for primers.

While we're on the subject, at some point you will need to decide which kind of paint to use: oil or latex (or acrylic). Some hobbyists prefer alkyds (synthetic oils). Most carvers today use tube acrylics but find that the gloss keeps the paint from "sticking." For years I have been painting my duck decoys and other bird carvings with latex exterior house paints, using bright acrylic tube colors for the reds, greens and yellows. This combination also works well on fish carvings. The only drawback for many hobbyists is that the minimum-size can of a flat latex house paint is a quart. If you plan to paint a number of decoys you can buy the quart cans and pour off a little at a time into smaller containers. The flat exterior latex colors I use are brown, black, white and rust red made by Cook & Dunn paints.

My personal preference for painting fish decoys is to use oil paints. Quality oils have a rich depth of color not obtainable with any other medium. Tube oils or artists' oils are fine.

For most fish carvings the paint scheme is roughly similar: a fairly solid base color along the top of the back, shading to a subtle wash of that color, to white on the underside. Color photographs of all but one of the carvings in this book, completed and painted, are shown on the covers. (The exception, the Lake Whitefish, is identical in coloration with the Round Whitefish; use the photograph of that carving as your guide.)

Experiment with different ways of applying paint to the carving. The "wet-on-wet" technique is one way of applying colors to your carving. This lets you blend colors with no discernible edge. "Dry-brushing" is a technique that I recommend in the painting suggestions that follow. It involves using the paint as it comes out of the tube, without any added linseed oil or turpentine (or without added water if you are using a water-based paint), and dabbing the brush against the carving, or "stippling." With practice, you will be able to create subtle effects similar to those obtainable with airbrushing. Experiment with different-size brushes, too. Fine-tipped brushes will allow you to add the smallest markings, including delicate scale edges, if you wish. Develop your technique so that your carvings are a reflection of your individual abilities.

Let's go through the procedure for painting one fish decoy, that of a northern pike. This will give you an idea of how to go about painting any of these carvings. Look at Fig. 8. After you have coated the unfinished carving with primer, as described

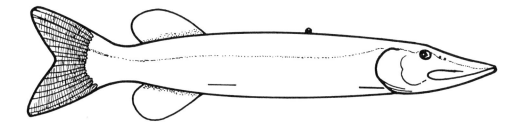

*Fig. 8.* Painting: Stage 1

above, paint the body white if necessary (most primers are already white; you may wish to add another coat). You generally would not want to paint the copper fins on a decoy—the natural copper color adds to the style of the work—so we will leave the fins alone, except for a few streaks. The caudal fin—better known as the tail!—is usually carved of wood, however, and in that case should be painted. Paint the tail of the pike with a rust red or red oxide paint. This completes stage one.

When the paint has dried thoroughly, you may proceed to stage two. Mix some raw sienna with Hooker's green (but keep the mixture very dry). Use a dry-brush technique to stipple the color in the area shown in Fig. 9. The top part of this area, from the gill covers back to the tail, should be darkest; stipple so the color fades as you work downward toward the ventral, or belly, area. While this is drying, mix burnt umber with black, and paint the dark streaks on the fins. Allow the paint to dry thoroughly before proceeding to stage three.

Mix black and Hooker's green, and paint along the dorsal area (that is, the back) from the base of the tail, over the head, to the tip of the mouth. Refer to Fig. 10. Lighten this dark green as you reach the sides of the fish, but let it be relatively dark on most of the head in front of the gill covers, except for a triangular area

between the eye and the mouth. When you are satisfied that the shading is just right, and the paint has dried, take a small brush and paint in white the bean-shaped marks that are the field mark of this popular game fish. Finally, inspect the area where the green paint runs into the white on the belly. If necessary, touch up this area to achieve a gradual shading.

Though I stopped at this point in my own painting of a northern pike, you may wish to add even finer detail—in particular, scales. Scale edges should be painted in thin lines with a fine brush in a slightly lighter or darker shade of the predominant color of the area you are covering. For example, when painting scales over a lighter area of your northern pike decoy, start with the original paint mixture you used for that area but blend in some green and burnt umber. I took this general approach in my own painting of the walleye, bluegill, largemouth bass and cisco decoys shown on the covers of this book.

In time you will gain facility and develop your own personal style. There are as many paint styles as there are painters, and that is a good thing. But success takes practice and patience. Now you can use the basics I have provided here as a foundation and—get going!

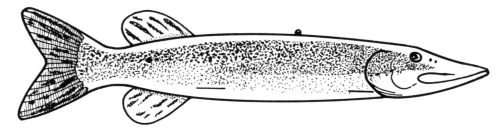

*Fig. 9.* Painting: Stage 2

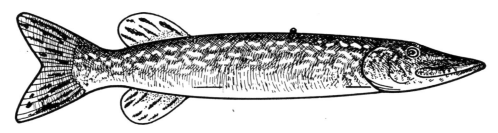

*Fig. 10.* Painting: Stage 3